Striped Animals

Teddy Borth

abdopublishing.com

Published by Abdo Kids, a division of ABDO, PO Box 398166, Minneapolis, Minnesota 55439.
Copyright © 2017 by Abdo Consulting Group, Inc. International copyrights reserved in all countries.
No part of this book may be reproduced in any form without written permission from the publisher.

Printed in the United States of America, North Mankato, Minnesota.

052016

092016

 THIS BOOK CONTAINS
RECYCLED MATERIALS

Photo Credits: iStock, Shutterstock

Production Contributors: Teddy Borth, Jennie Forsberg, Grace Hansen

Design Contributors: Christina Doffing, Candice Keimig, Dorothy Toth

Cataloging-in-Publication Data

Names: Borth, Teddy, author.

Title: Striped animals / by Teddy Borth.

Description: Minneapolis, MN : Abdo Kids, [2017] | Series: Animal skins |
    Includes bibliographical references and index.

Identifiers: LCCN 2015959005 | ISBN 9781680804980 (lib. bdg.) |
    ISBN 9781680805543 (ebook) | ISBN 9781680806106 (Read-to-me ebook)

Subjects: LCSH: Body Covering (Anatomy)--Juvenile literature. | Skin--Juvenile
    literature.

Classification: DDC 591.47--dc23

LC record available at http://lccn.loc.gov/2015959005

Table of Contents

Striped Animals

Animals have skin!

There are many kinds.

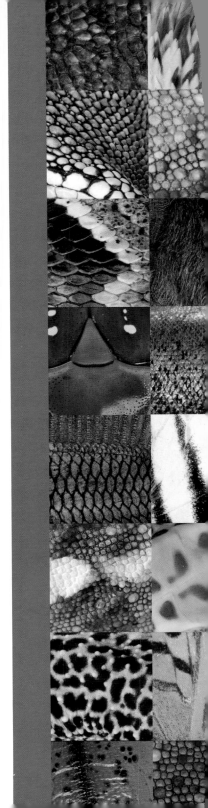

Some animals have stripes.

They have lines on their bodies.

bongo

Stripes can be on fur.

They can be on scales.

They can be on bugs.

blue ring angelfish

9

Zebras have them. They keep flies away.

zebra

Tigers have them.

They use them to hide.

This lets them hunt.

tiger

Some animals hide to stay safe.

chipmunk

15

Stripes can mean danger.
Bees use them. Birds know
to stay away!

bumblebee

Snakes use them.

They warn of **poison**.

coral snake

A skunk sprays a bad smell. Its stripes warn you. Do not get too close!

skunk

Other Striped Animals

mackerel tabby cat

okapi

numbat

raccoon

Glossary

danger
the chance of coming into contact
with harm or injury.

fur
the short, fine hair of
certain animals.

poison
a substance that can cause
illness or death.

Index

abdokids.com

Use this code to log on to abdokids.com and access crafts, games, videos, and more!

Abdo Kids Code:
ASK4980